The
COLUMBUS
Project Book NPT

DAVID McDOWALL

Project Consultant:
Valerie Nott

eadway · Hodder & Stoughton

Landfall America

When we speak of America today, many of us think of a land of fast food, high buildings and wide highways. It all looked very different to Christopher Columbus when he arrived by ship five hundred years ago.

His first reaction must have been one of huge relief. After sailing without sight of land for thirty-two days, his men had wanted to turn back while they still had enough food and water to reach Spain. They feared they would die if they went on.

However, Columbus persuaded them to go on for just three more days, and on 11 October 1492, when his three days were up, they saw flocks of birds, a hand-carved stick and part of a flowering shrub floating in the water. Excited, they decided to go on, and at 2 am that night, the man on watch cried 'Land ahoy!' He had sighted America!

They did not approach the shore until dawn, in case of rocks hidden in the darkness. From their ships they saw a sandy beach fringed by beautiful palm trees. Pelicans walked along the shore, and monkeys climbed in the trees.

Then the inhabitants appeared, and were astonished!

A Spaniard of the time described the encounter:

> The natives, of whom there was a large number, gazed dumbstruck at the Christians, looking with wonder at their beards, their clothes and the whiteness of their skin . . . They touched the men's beards with their fingers and carefully examined the paleness of their hands and faces. Seeing that they were innocent, the admiral and his men did not resist their actions.

The first thing the Spaniards noticed was that the inhabitants were naked.

Neither Columbus, nor any of his comrades, thought that they had found a new continent. Columbus had wanted to find the 'Indies' – by which he meant South East Asia, the region from India around to China. He remained convinced he had indeed found the 'Indies'. As a result, he and all other Europeans called the inhabitants 'Indians', and the islands he found continued to be known as the West Indies.

Merchants bringing goods from the East on camels

TAKE IT FROM HERE

1 Make a photo montage of America today. Collect pictures, postcards, tourist material and adverts. If done well, you'll soon have a lovely poster for your room.

2 Find out about life aboard ship during the fifteenth century. What would the crew have had to eat and drink, how were these items stored and how long would they have lasted before becoming unfit for consumption?

3 In good weather, when the ship was not rolling, a meal was cooked on a wood fire made in an iron box with a layer of sand and earth in the bottom. Get an adult to help you make a wood fire out of doors and use it to cook a meal.

4 You can travel to America a good deal more quickly now than Columbus did. Check whether you can still go by ship. Find out how long it takes and compare it with the time of an air flight.

5 Make a 'New World' fruit salad with whichever American ingredients are locally available: for example, sugar cane, bananas, avocado, custard apples, pineapples, pawpaw (or papaya).

Europe and the search for the Indies

The port of Genoa from a seventeenth century oil painting

Why was Columbus so anxious to find the Indies? The answer lies partly in the Mediterranean. The great Italian city of Genoa had one of the largest fleets in the Mediterranean and had become rich by trading with the Muslims at its eastern end. Genoese merchants sold the Muslims **alum** (a substance used in textile production for fixing dyes) and also white slaves whom they brought from the Black Sea area, for service in the great Muslim houses and palaces.

In return, they bought silks and spices, which were in great demand in Europe. Some of these came from Muslim lands, but most came from 'the Indies' beyond – India, the 'Spice Islands' (Indonesia) and China.

Silks and spices fetched a very high price in Europe. Silks were worn by the very rich, and spices were used to improve the taste of meat. This was important as most animals in north Europe were killed in winter because there was not enough food to keep whole flocks alive. Salt and spices prevented meat from going bad and also disguised the bad taste of stale meat.

In order to carry on this trade, Genoese ships had to be able to sail freely in the eastern Mediterranean and to the Black Sea. In 1453, the Muslim Turks captured the ancient Christian city of Constantinople and closed the Black Sea route.

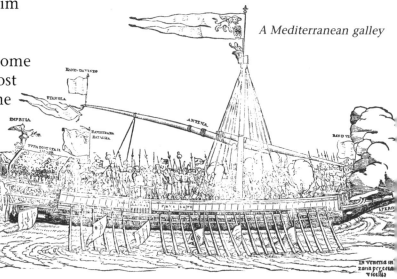

A Mediterranean galley

The siege of Constantinople in 1453

It was not long before Genoese sailors **enrolled** on Portuguese ships. One of these sailors was Christopher Columbus. He had been born in Genoa in 1451 and began his career as a sailor at the age of eight in 1459. But, by the mid 1470s, he felt he had no future in Genoa, and went to Lisbon and began sailing on Portuguese ships, and in the words of his first **biographer**, he 'often sailed with the Portuguese as if he had been one of them'.

Over the next twenty years the Genoese were pushed out of the eastern Mediterranean, as the Turks took over the trade themselves, and the Muslim pirates attacked their ships.

It was clear that Genoa's wealth would be destroyed if it could not find an independent route to the Indies, so that it could trade freely. Genoese bankers therefore decided to finance exploration outside the Mediterranean in order to find such a route. A country that was already involved in exploration was the one which was closest to Africa and the Atlantic: Portugal.

TAKE IT FROM HERE

1 Cloves, nutmeg, mace, cinnamon and cardamom all come from the East Indies (Indonesia and neighbouring countries). Ask an adult if you have any in the kitchen cupboard, and learn to recognise the smell of these spices. With adult help, make a Christmas cake or a pudding using spices.

2 Try making your own natural dye. You will need:
   50 g alum (from a craft shop or large chemist)
   40 g cream of tartar
   20 g cochineal
   White cotton (or wool), for example, an old handkerchief or pillow case
   Dissolve the alum and cream of tartar in a small amount of water, add 8 pints and then the cochineal. Wet the cloth, then immerse it in the mixture. Simmer over a gentle heat for an hour, or longer if you want a darker shade. Leave to cool in the mixture, then rinse thoroughly and dry. Try other colours: onion skins for yellow; elderberry for red; sunflower seeds for blue; coffee for beige; oak leaves for autumn colours.

3 Which other famous Italian port once rivalled Genoa's sea trade?

4 What is Constantinople's modern name?

5 Ask your local junior librarian to find you a book about the Turkish Empire and the capture of Constantinople.

Portugal's development of ships and navigation

Portugal was on the edge of Europe. It was mountainous and agriculturally poor, but it lived off the sea: fishing and trading. Until the fifteenth century, this was done mainly in coastal waters, because neither ocean-going ships nor adequate **navigation** skills had been developed.

In the early fifteenth century, Portugal's ruler, Prince Henry, wanted to explore the coastline of Africa and discover a sea route to the 'Indies'. He encouraged the design of ships suitable for exploration. These were called 'caravels'. The larger of the caravels usually had 'square' sails hung across the boat to catch wind from behind, and also 'lateen' sails, which were hung in line with the **hull**, or body, of the boat, as in the case of modern sailing boats. If the wind dropped completely, these ships could be propelled by very long oars. This was the kind of ship which Columbus used.

Prince Henry was nicknamed 'The Navigator' because he founded a school of navigation for exploration of the oceans. For forty years, helped by Arab and Jewish geographers and mappers (who knew more about exploration, navigation and astronomy than the Europeans), Henry sent expeditions to Madeira (1420), the Canaries (which were already known) and the Azores (1431–1444), and the uninhabited Cape Verde Islands (1446) and the mainland African coast beyond.

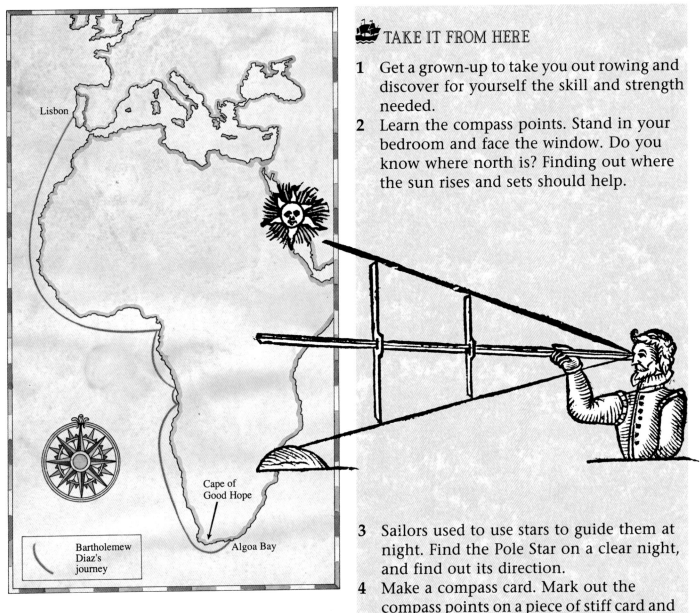

Lisbon

Cape of
Good Hope

Algoa Bay

Bartholemew
Diaz's
journey

TAKE IT FROM HERE

1 Get a grown-up to take you out rowing and discover for yourself the skill and strength needed.

2 Learn the compass points. Stand in your bedroom and face the window. Do you know where north is? Finding out where the sun rises and sets should help.

3 Sailors used to use stars to guide them at night. Find the Pole Star on a clear night, and find out its direction.

4 Make a compass card. Mark out the compass points on a piece of stiff card and put a long nail or pin in the centre. Put it out in the sun, and the shadow will touch north at noon.

5 Find out about the sun. (Do not look straight at the sun as it will damage your eyes.) Why does the height of the sun vary in summer and winter? In which season does the sun appear lower in the sky? How does this affect the hours of daylight and the climate?

6 Look at a globe or a world atlas. Find the lines of **latitude** (running west–east) and **longitude** (running north–south). Look carefully. In what way are these lines obviously different?

Exploring the West Africa coast, seafarers realised that they could tell their **latitude** (how far north or south they were from the Equator) from the height of the midday sun (the **zenith**) above the horizon. Since the sun is at a slightly different height each day of the year, a book of tables was produced telling sea captains the daily zenith at any particular latitude, north or south of the Equator.

In 1488, armed with these tables, Bartholemew Diaz, an explorer, rounded the southern tip of Africa, reaching just beyond the Cape of Good Hope. He then turned back, convinced he had found the route to India.

Mapping the world

Why was Columbus so sure in 1492 that he had found the Indies? Why did he think he had got there by sailing westwards?

It was partly because of the knowledge that the world was, in fact, round – rather than flat, as had earlier been thought. Educated people now knew that it was round by study of the stars, and also because ships always disappeared 'below' the horizon, or came 'up' over the horizon. This could only be explained by the curve of the earth's surface.

During the fifteenth century, there was a rediscovery of the geographical work of the Ancient World. As early as AD 130 the Egyptian, Ptolemy, had mapped the Roman Empire and neighbouring areas, but he had filled in the rest of the world with imaginary lands, arguing that Africa and China were joined to a southern land mass, leaving the Indian Ocean surrounded by land. If this were true, it might be easier to sail *west* to China, than to try to cross Africa and this 'southern land mass'. Ptolemy also reckoned the globe was smaller than it really is. True or false,

Columbus saw the difficulty the Portuguese had in sailing beyond Africa, and decided that the westerly route would be easier.

Fifteenth century scholars were little better informed than Ptolemy. In 1474, an Italian scholar, Paul Toscanelli, advised the Portuguese that the shortest route to the Indies was to sail westwards. His map is shown below.

Like Ptolemy, Toscanelli underestimated the **circumference** of the globe. Columbus almost certainly saw Toscanelli's map, and probably copied it. At any rate, Columbus decided that the globe was even smaller than Ptolemy and Toscanelli had thought – only three-quarters of its actual size. He made another big mistake. He thought that China extended far further eastwards than it actually does. Both these mistakes led him to think that his journey would be far shorter. He would never have reached China, but would have died of thirst and hunger long before. He was lucky to reach land first, even if he failed to recognise that it was, in fact, a 'New World'.

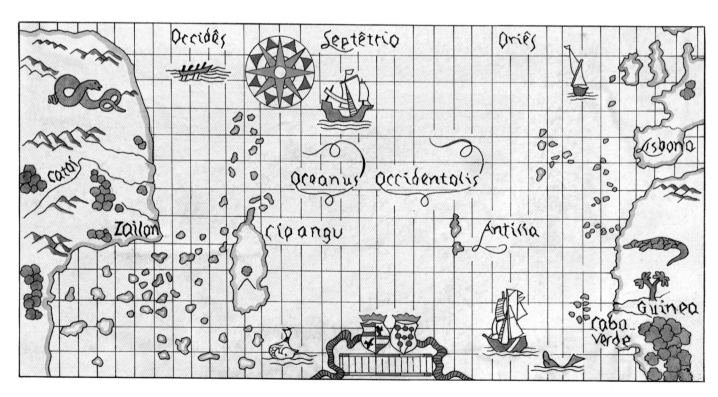

TAKE IT FROM HERE

1 Mappers used to have to draw what they had not seen, trusting travellers, seafaring experience and the stars. You have probably seen a map of the world (or Great Britain). Try drawing it from memory. Then compare it with an atlas to see how much you really know. Get a friend to draw a map of an island, without showing you, and then ask them to describe it to you. See if you can draw it from the description.

2 There are over 150 countries in the world today. Challenge a few friends to write down as many as they can think of, first in Europe, then in America.

3 Try to measure the world's **circumference** from a map or a globe, using a piece of thread or a ruler, and checking it against the scale. If necessary, get an adult to help you.

4 Compare Toscanelli's map with a modern one.

Columbus sets sail

and that he had greatly underestimated both the size of the world, and the percentage of the earth's surface which was ocean.

In the meantime, Columbus tried to interest the kings of France and England in financing the voyage, but without success. No one was interested.

Then, Columbus's luck changed. In the summer of 1492, Queen Isabella changed her mind, and decided to finance an expedition of three ships: the Santa Maria; and two lighter caravels, the Nina and Pinta. Columbus sailed from the port of Palos on 3 August, reaching the Canary Islands on 8 August. On 6 September, he set out to cross the Atlantic, reaching an island he called San Salvador (now called Watling Island) in the West Indies on 12 October.

Columbus bids farewell to Queen Isabella and King Ferdinand

In 1483, Columbus tried to persuade the Portuguese king to finance a voyage to discover the Indies by the westerly route. If his theory was right, that the Indies could be reached more easily by sailing westwards, the Portuguese would have wasted a century of navigation trying to find an easterly route beyond the southern tip of Africa. But the king was no more convinced than he had been by Toscanelli's map nine years earlier. The following year Columbus went to Spain, hoping for royal support.

The two Spanish kingdoms of Aragon and Castile had just been united, by the marriage of King Ferdinand (Aragon) and Queen Isabella (Castile). Both wanted to compete with Portugal in exploration and trading. Having met Columbus, they sought expert advice about his theories. In 1490, these experts reported correctly that the distance to the Indies was far greater than Columbus claimed,

Columbus was certain that he had reached islands on the edge of Asia. Everything fitted his theory. The only problem was that there were no fabulous cities to be found – only forests and tribespeople.

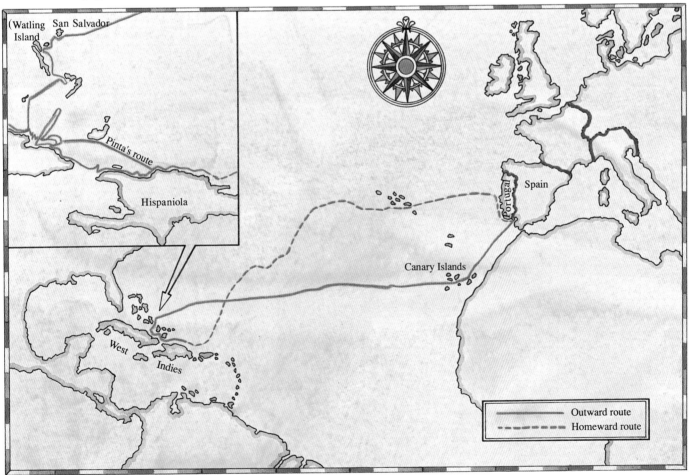

TAKE IT FROM HERE

1 One reason why Ferdinand and Isabella took so long to decide about Columbus was that they were busy fighting a war within Spain. Find out who they were fighting, and what happened.
2 Would *you* have paid for Columbus to carry out his expedition to find the Indies by sailing westwards? List the points for, and against, paying for the voyage.
3 If you were Columbus, what promises of reward would you have asked for if your expedition proved successful?
4 Imagine you are Columbus. Design the flags you would wish to fly. Put them up in your bedroom.

Columbus's voyage in 1492

(Watling Island   San Salvador

Pinta's route

Hispaniola

West Indies

Portugal   Spain

Canary Islands

—————— Outward route
– – – – – – Homeward route

What Columbus found

The inhabitants of the islands were cautious but friendly. Amongst many things, Columbus noticed that they smoked rolled-up leaves (tobacco), and they slept in hammocks. Both ideas were entirely new to Europeans. Even more interesting to them were the gold ornaments that the people wore. They learned that the gold came from a larger island called Cuba and Columbus set off at once, thinking it must be Cipangu, or Japan. However, he found little gold on Cuba, and sailed on to an island he called 'Little Spain', or Hispaniola (today's Haiti/Dominica).

The inhabitants of Hispaniola told him that beyond the island was a large continent – the land of the Caribs, terrible man-eating enemies. Columbus decided that this was China, and the Caribs must be Chinese pirates. By this time, Columbus and his men were anxious to find out just one thing: where the gold came from.

Since he had so few men and was running out of supplies, Columbus felt unable to continue his search for gold for the present. He decided to return to Spain to report his findings. However, before he could do so, the Santa Maria was wrecked on the rocky shore of Hispaniola. It would have been too crowded to carry all the men on the Nina and Pinta, so Columbus left thirty-nine of them behind in a fort made of the Santa Maria's timbers.

TAKE IT FROM HERE

1 Columbus found brightly coloured birds in the West Indies. Make a collage of a parrot. First, draw the outline of a parrot, then cut out feather shapes from brightly coloured tissue or art paper and glue them on, starting at the bottom and working up, to get a feather effect.

2 Why do people smoke tobacco? How does it damage their health? Make an anti-smoking poster.

3 Pretend you are Columbus leaving some of your men behind on the island. Either tell a group of friends, or write down your instructions. Consider the need to keep order and good behaviour; to stay on friendly terms with the local inhabitants; to provide for daily food and water; to stay alert and safe in case the locals became unfriendly.

4 Who do you think owned the islands that Columbus discovered? Do you think he should have made an agreement with the local people to allow some of his men to stay? With a friend playing the part of Columbus, pretend you are the local village chief, and agree on suitable conditions for both the locals and the crew.

Getting home

Columbus had crossed the Atlantic using the south-easterly winds and currents from the Canaries. On his way back, he knew enough about the Atlantic to realise that he had to pick up the 'westerlies' (winds are always described by the direction they are blowing *from*) which blew further north. So he sailed until he was as far north as Bermuda before striking eastwards. Recrossing the Atlantic, the Nina and Pinta covered more than 100 miles a day, but no one had much idea of where exactly they were!

Prevailing winds

Then things began to go wrong. Columbus wrote in the log: 'the sea began to swell and the sky grew stormy . . . we could neither advance nor make our way out of the waves attacking the caravels and breaking against them . . . if the caravels had not been very good ships and well repaired, they would surely have been lost.'

The crew prayed for deliverance. Although neither ship was sunk in the storm, the Nina was driven out of sight of the other crew, and Columbus, on the Pinta, was driven into Lisbon for shelter. It was embarrassing, having to explain to the Portuguese king that he had just found the Indies for Portugal's great rival, Spain – and that he had done so by going west. Fortunately, the king, though very suspicious, did not believe the story and let Columbus go.

Columbus reached Palos on 15 March 1493, and travelled triumphantly to the court in Barcelona where the entire city and court came out to welcome him.

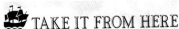 TAKE IT FROM HERE

1 Lick a finger and hold it up to the wind. The side which feels cold is the side the wind is blowing from. Try to tell from where the wind is blowing, with a compass.
2 Fly a kite and feel the strength of the wind.
3 Look at a weather-chart in a newspaper, and ask an adult to help explain it.
4 Find out what the different jobs at sea entail. For example, a caulker keeps the ship watertight; a steward is in charge of supplies and stores. What about a pilot or mate? Joiner? Sailmaker?

5 Measuring time at sea used to be done with an hourglass. The ship's boy had to watch it and turn it. Make an hourglass of your own, from two identical plastic bottles with screw tops and some fine sand. Make small holes in the plastic caps. Put enough sand in a bottle to take, say, ten minutes to run out into the other bottle. Increase the size of hole if necessary. Once accurate, sellotape the two bottles together so that the sand runs from one bottle to the other. Fix into a cardboard box for stability. Every time the hourglass empties, you must turn it over.
6 Write a poem about a storm at sea.
7 Make a newspaper, reporting details of the discovery of America, and including a feature article on Columbus's request for a second expedition and how you think Ferdinand and Isabella will respond.

Columbus's second and third voyages

It was not long before Columbus, too, found himself fighting the inhabitants. He sent 500 captives to Spain as slaves, 200 of whom died shortly after reaching the country. Then he taxed the inhabitants, as a way of getting them to hand over gold, but they ran away into the hills and began attacking the Spanish.

Just as he was about to set sail home from Hispaniola, a **hurricane** (a word of the inhabitants) destroyed most of his ships. Luckily, everyone was still ashore. Columbus told those he could not take to find a suitable site for a city. Then he set sail with his two remaining ships, reaching Cadiz in June 1496. This time, nobody turned out to greet him. Columbus had returned with very little gold. No one was pleased, and he had great difficulty getting support for a third journey. (He claimed that Cuba was the Malay Peninsula, running down from the Asian mainland.) He warned that if he was not allowed to sail back, the Portuguese might get there first. Eventually, he got his permission, and sailed in 1498.

This time, Columbus reached the South American mainland, the coast of present-day Venezuela, where the inhabitants wore large pearls on their arms. He realised that he was on the edge of a continent, but thought it was China. On the southern side of Hispaniola he found that the men he had left behind the second time had begun to build a city – what was to become Santo Domingo.

Columbus led a second expedition, with 17 ships and 1200 men. He planned to search for gold, and also to settle farmers on the fertile land he had seen. So he took seed for cereals and animals to breed from. He left Cadiz in September 1493.

This voyage was beset with disasters. When he reached Hispaniola, Columbus found nothing left of the fort except ashes, rubbish, and a few decayed bodies. It was difficult to be sure what had happened, but it seemed that the men he had left behind had quarrelled amongst themselves and then upset the local people by taking some of their women. As a result, they were attacked and killed.

Columbus began to quarrel with some of the Spanish settlers, who disliked having a Genoese as their Governor. His letters back to Spain showed that he had managed his men badly, had unrealistic expectations of what he could achieve and was unable to take advice. Ferdinand and Isabella decided to send out a

Governor to replace him. The new Governor found that Columbus had started hanging those settlers who opposed him and in 1500 Columbus was sent back to Spain in disgrace.

A gold mask and pendant from the Inca civilization (see page 23)

 TAKE IT FROM HERE

1 What makes gold precious? Is it heavier or lighter than most metals? Does it tarnish (lose its **lustre** or shine)?
2 Draw a map of a large island, putting in imaginary mountains, rivers and forests, and villages of the inhabitants. Now site your own settlement. Keep in mind the need for fresh water (from spring or river), safe anchorage for your ships, and land where you could grow food or keep animals.
3 Find out how pearls are made.
4 Find Venezuela and Santo Domingo on a map.
5 Find Malaysia (Malay Peninsula) on a map and see how far away it is from Cuba, which Columbus thought was Malaysia.

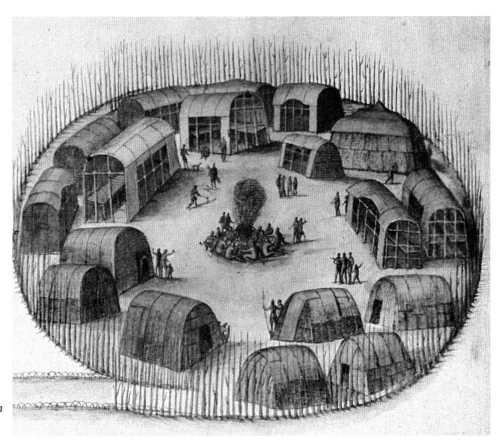

Discontent in an Indian village at the arrival of the Spanish

The final journey

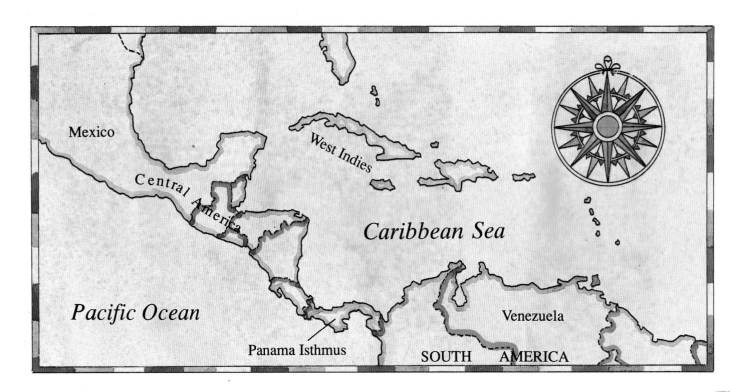

In spite of his disgrace, Columbus convinced Ferdinand and Isabella that although others had now explored south and north of the islands he had discovered, no one had explored the sea directly west of them. That was where, he argued, the westward passage to the Indies must be. He got permission to explore, but only on condition that he did not go near Hispaniola. Ferdinand and Isabella did not want more trouble between him and the Spanish settlers. They told him to bring back gold, silver, pearls, precious stones and spices.

Columbus sailed to the Central American coast in 1502 and discovered from the inhabitants that this was an **isthmus** (a narrow neck of land). He was not equipped to cross the land to the Pacific and, in any case, he still thought he was somewhere on the Malay Peninsula. He managed to found a gold mine, but the climate, the soil, and the attacks of the inhabitants made it too difficult to mine the gold.

When Colombus set sail again, he found that his ships had been attacked by shipworms, which burrowed through the hulls, letting the water in. By a miracle, he managed to reach Jamaica, and, with the help of local inhabitants, two canoes were built and sailed to Santo Domingo on the south side of Hispaniola to organise a rescue party. The journey took almost five weeks, but nine months passed before the Spanish in Santo Domingo rescued Columbus.

When he got back to Spain he found the queen was dying. The king had had enough of Columbus and refused to see him. Columbus began to complain that he was being badly treated by the king, and demanded money. But everyone had lost patience with him. He died, more or less forgotten, in 1506.

TAKE IT FROM HERE

1 Look at a map of Central America. See if you can find the canal which has been dug through one of the countries on the isthmus, from the Atlantic to the Pacific.
2 Archaeologists have discovered stone masks in Central America. Make your own mask. Try, for example, making a mould of your face with foil, and then backing it carefully with papier mâché.
3 Pretend you are Columbus and write a letter to the king, arguing for a better reward. Get a friend to reply, as king.
4 Find and draw the Spanish royal arms. Find out which parts are the badges of Castile and Aragon.
5 Draw your own coat of arms which says something about who you are, where you live or what your interests are.

Indians panning for gold

The first to cross the Atlantic

Columbus was certainly not the first European to reach America. Five hundred years earlier, Viking ships had made the crossing, taking an easier route: Norway – Shetland – Faroes – Iceland – Greenland – Baffin Island – Labrador – Massachusetts.

They had ships which were lighter and faster than any ships of similar size, and were beautifully designed. When a replica Viking ship sailed across the Atlantic a century ago, in 1893, its captain said: 'the finest merchant ships of our day . . . have practically the same type of bottom as the Viking ships.'

Why did the Vikings travel to North America?

Norway had little fertile land. As the population grew, Vikings set out to settle in other places. Some settled on the north and east coasts of Britain, others on the north coast of France. A few founded settlements in Iceland and Greenland.

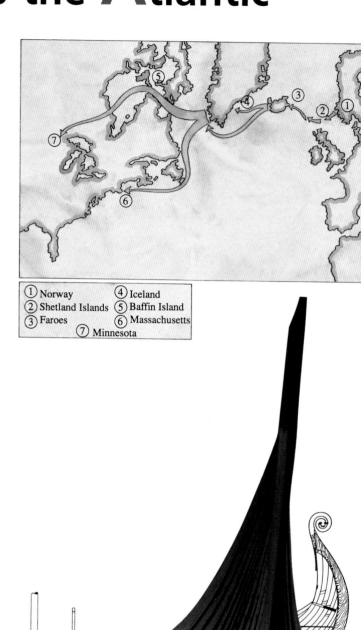

① Norway	④ Iceland
② Shetland Islands	⑤ Baffin Island
③ Faroes	⑥ Massachusetts
⑦ Minnesota	

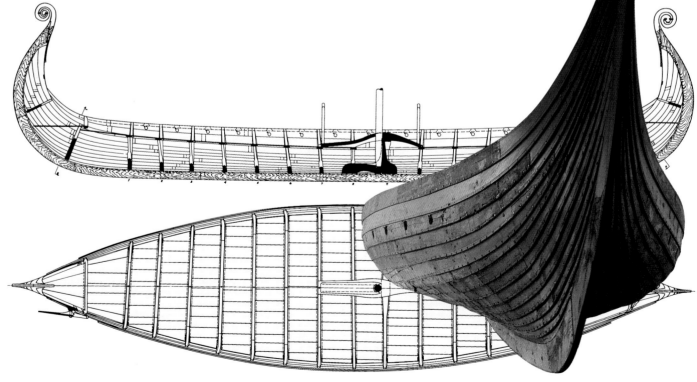

The first Viking ship probably reached North America in 986, but the most famous journey was made by Leif Erikson in 1003. He made his way across from Greenland, down the Labrador coast to Nantucket, Massachusetts.

Why didn't the Vikings settle in Massachusetts? It is likely that they tried to, but the inhabitants – whom they called 'skraelings' – probably attacked them, making it impossible to grow food or protect their animals.

The Vikings did not think they were the first to cross the Atlantic. They believed that the Irish had made the crossing before them, in large fishing boats, in about AD 850 – over a century before them.

 **TAKE IT FROM HERE**

1. Which sort of ship would you prefer to travel in – Columbus's caravel or the Viking longship? Consider the sails, the shape of the boat, the oars and storage space available.
2. Model a longship using Plasticine or Playdough for the hull, and sticks for the mast and oars. Cut a piece of paper or cloth for the sail and find a Viking motif to paint on it.
3. If you are close enough, go to see the Viking remains at the Jorvik Centre, York, or in the British Museum, London.
4. What is the capital of Ireland? Who founded it?
5. Find out which British islands were once ruled by the Vikings.

Saint Brendan, the Irish monk, who was thought to have crossed the Atlantic in the ninth century

America's first settlers

However, neither the Irish nor the Vikings were the first people to *discover* America. The first people to reach America did so about 30,000 years ago, during the Ice Age. A fall in the sea level meant it was possible to walk on dry land from Siberia (in today's Soviet Union) to Alaska. Small bands of Siberian hunters followed the animals they hunted into the other continent. Gradually, they spread over the whole continent, reaching South America by about 12,000 BC. By the time of Columbus, there were more than 30 million people living in the Americas, and as many as 600 different languages were spoken.

Most of them, perhaps 25 million, lived in Mexico, where they had a highly developed agriculture. Nearly half the foods grown in the world today were first grown by these inhabitants – the 'Amerindians', as they became known. Both north and south of Mexico, most Amerindian groups lived by fishing, hunting and gathering wild fruits, nuts, roots and vegetables, like the North American Indians.

Aztec civilization

Maya civilization

Inca civilization

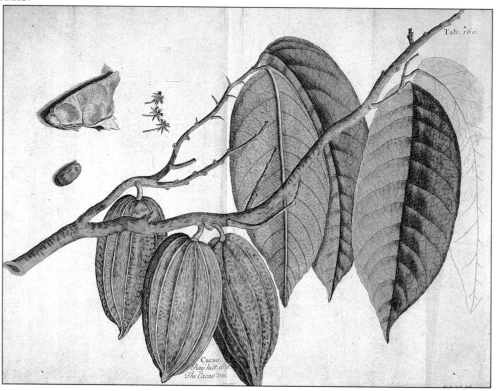

Leaves and bean-pods of cacao, from which cocoa and chocolate are made

American Civilizations

There were three great American civilizations when Columbus reached America.

The largest was the **Aztec** Empire, which covered all present-day Mexico. The Aztecs built great pyramids – almost certainly with slave labour – and had a system of pictographs for writing. Curiously, they used metal only for ornaments – all their tools and weapons were made of stone, flint or **obsidian** (a hard, sharp rock like black glass). They also practised human sacrifice.

Remains of buildings from the Aztec Empire

In the Andes mountains (present-day Peru, Chile and Bolivia), was the **Inca** civilization. The Incas had a wonderful agricultural system in the mountains, with **irrigation** channels to water the crops, which were grown on levelled 'steps', or terraces, on the mountainsides.

In present-day Honduras and Guatemala, lived the **Maya** civilization. For 600 years, between AD 300–900, the Mayas had the most advanced mathematicians and astronomers in the world. They also built magnificent buildings.

Elsewhere, there were less developed groups. The first people Columbus met were **Tainos** and **Arawaks**, of whom none now survive. On other islands, and on the mainland, he met **Caribs** – a fiercer people who ate human flesh.

TAKE IT FROM HERE

1 Chocolate beans come from America, where they were highly prized as a food and sometimes used as money. With adult help, try melting some cooking chocolate in a saucepan over boiling water. When it is melted, dip plain biscuits in, and put them on a wire tray to cool.

2 Columbus discovered Capsicum peppers. Grow a red or green pepper on your windowsill. Tomatoes and potatoes also come from America. Make a salad using all these ingredients.

3 Look at a book on 'pre-Columban' civilizations in the library. Look at illustrations of jewellery. Make your own 'gold' jewellery with gold or silver foil, scrap paper, wallpaper paste, leather bootlaces, string, bits of pasta, card, safety pins. Make papier mâché shapes, and dry them. (Leave holes to string them by.) Stick on pieces of pasta and string, and cover with foil. Try making bracelets or headbands.

4 Create your own pictograph story depicting Columbus's first voyage like the one below.

The clash of cultures: first impressions

When they first met, both the Amerindians and the Europeans discovered in each other a new kind of human being that they had never imagined. As we know from Columbus's log, the immediate European picture was that the inhabitants were naked, childlike and defenceless against European weapons.

On his first voyage, Columbus wrote:

> Your Highnesses [Ferdinand and Isabella] should know that this island [Hispaniola], and all the others, belong to you as much as Castile does. To rule here, one need only get settled and exercise authority over the natives, who will carry out whatever they are ordered to do. I, with my crew – a bare handful of men – could conquer all these islands with no resistance whatever. The Indians always run away; they have no weapons, nor the warring spirit. They are naked and defenceless, thus ready to be given orders and put to work.

He thought they would easily be made Christian, 'since it appears they have no religion of their own . . . I think that Christendom [the Christian countries] will do good business with these Indians, especially Spain, whose subjects they must all become'.

From Mexico to Peru, the inhabitants were struck by the characteristics of the Europeans: their white skin, their beards, their horses and weapons and finally their writing.

This is what the Aztec king was told about the Spanish invaders:

> Their bodies are completely covered up, only their faces can be seen, and these are as white as chalk. They have yellow hair, although in some cases it is black. Their beards are long, and their moustaches are also yellow . . . They are mounted on their 'stags' [horses]. Perched in this way, they ride at rooftop level. If the shot [of a cannon] touches a hill, it seems to split it, to crack it open.

An Aztec meets Spanish soldiers

Montezuma, ruler of the Aztecs, hears a description of the Spaniards

An Aztec head-dress

The Amerindians also believed that the Spanish were Gods. This is how some Amerindians saw them:

They saw them mounted on huge animals with feet of silver. They saw that they were able to talk to each other without difficulty, by means of white cloth.

But the idea that the Europeans were Gods was quickly spoilt when they saw the Europeans' greed for gold:

They picked up the gold and fingered it like monkeys . . . their bodies swell with greed. They hungered like pigs for that gold.

TAKE IT FROM HERE

1 The Aztecs made stone mosaics. Design your own decorative mosaic, by cutting out squares of coloured paper.
2 What were the 'feet of silver', and 'pieces of white cloth' which the Amerindians spoke of?
3 Allspice, chilli, tabasco and paprika all come from America. Ask an adult to help you cook dishes using these. Some are *very hot*, so be careful! Try a Mexican recipe. Taco shells are available at many supermarkets. Make a meat, onion and pepper mixture to stuff the tacos.

The conquest of Central and South America

Atlantic Ocean

Aztec Mexico
conquered 1519-21

Area from Honduras to
Eastern tip of
Brazil explored
by 1508

Yucatan Peninsula
conquered 1545

Panama Isthmus
crossed and
Pacific Ocean
reached 1513

Inca Peru
conquered
1533-48

Pacific Ocean

River Plate
discovered 1516

There were three main reasons for European conquest. The immediate reason was the greed for gold, silver and other precious minerals. But there was also the desire for land on which to settle Spain's growing population, and a growing need for slaves to work in the gold mines and on the farms the Spanish established. The Spanish found that the Amerindian slaves died very quickly from mistreatment and disease and so they conquered more areas to capture more slaves and when these died, the Spanish went in search of more. Amerindian tribes often helped the Europeans against enemy tribes, and this made European conquest far easier.

The Brazilian rain forest before deforestation (below left) and after deforestation (below)

Amerindians were driven off the most fertile land to make way for European farms. They were also forced to give up their old religious beliefs, many of which were to do with living in harmony with the environment, and to accept Christianity.

The conquests were very rapid. Hispaniola, Cuba and most of the other West Indian islands were conquered within ten years. Almost the whole of Central America and the west coast of South America were conquered between 1492 and 1550 – a period of less than sixty years.

The Spanish conquerors also took Amerindian women. Their descendants were of mixed Spanish and Amerindian blood, and are known as **mestizos**. Most South and Central Americans are mestizos.

There are very few pure Amerindians left. They retreated from the Spanish into the jungles – for example, into the Amazon basin. They are still the object of conquest today. Farmers and businessmen continue to cut down their forests and drive them off their land, which they want to take for cattle ranching or mining. The demand for various metals has also led to the felling of jungle for mining; and increased cattle ranching is the result of increased demand for beef – especially for beefburgers and other forms of fast food which are in demand in many parts of the world.

The Brazilian rain forest, in which many Amerindians live, is being destroyed at a rate of 50 million acres a year. The Amerindians often have no one to defend them, and are the first to suffer. However, in the end, *everyone* suffers, because the destruction of the tropical rain forests of America damages the ecology (or natural balance) that makes our planet habitable.

🚢 TAKE IT FROM HERE

1 Native Americans used feathers for their head-dresses. Collect some feathers with your friends and make a simple head-dress, using a cardboard base.
2 The Aztecs sent messages using a **quipa**, a ring of wire hung with lengths of string knotted at various levels. No one now knows how to decipher this language. Make a quipa and create your own code.
3 Make a bracelet using card and foil.
4 Design greetings cards using Amerindian designs. They are easy to reproduce on squared paper.
5 Write to Survival International, 310 Edgware Road, London W2 1DY, and ask them to send you information about threatened Amerindian people.
6 Write to Friends of the Earth, 26–28 Underwood Street, London N1 7JQ, and ask for information concerning the destruction of the rain forests.

The conquest of North America

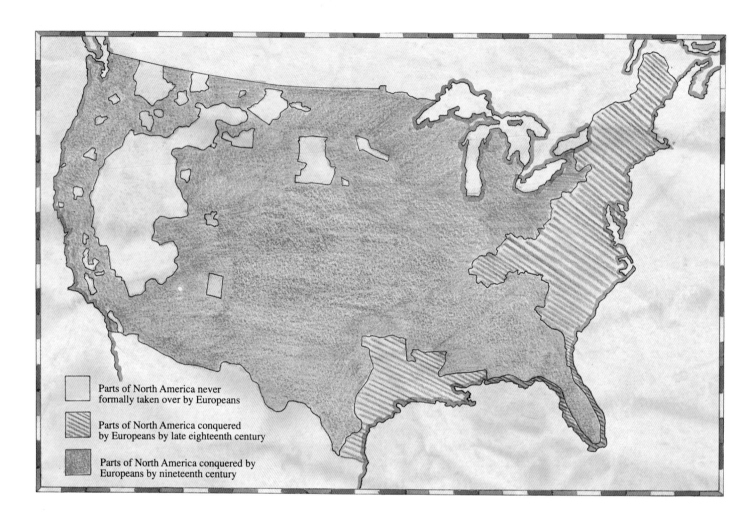

Parts of North America never
formally taken over by Europeans

Parts of North America conquered
by Europeans by late eighteenth century

Parts of North America conquered by
Europeans by nineteenth century

In North America, the conquests took far longer. At first, the mainly French and British colonists settled only in the east coast area. They did not interfere very much with the native Americans – they were too concerned with fighting each other. Indian tribes made alliances with one side or the other in the British–French wars. By 1776, the year in which the United States declared its independence, white settlers had not advanced beyond the Ohio River. The real conquests took place during the following century, when thousands of new white settlers pushed west to establish farms, find gold and lay railroads across to the west coast.

The native Americans had no real defence. They had never fought long wars. Wars between tribes had, in the past, generally been short-lived quarrels over animal pastures. But in the white man, the Indian faced an entirely new kind of enemy – one who was determined to conquer, and to destroy those who resisted him.

After 1776, the USA drove the Indians further and further west. Many chiefs resisted. If they had been able to unite as a single Indian nation they might have held the Whites back. But they fought independently, and one by one they were defeated. Some fled north to the safety of Canada, which – unlike the USA – kept its promises to the Indian tribes and generally treated them with some respect and fairness.

Only one Indian chief, Red Cloud of the Oglala Sioux, won a war (1865–8) against the US Government. He made peace and obtained creation of the Great Sioux Reservation in Nebraska. Others fought on and were defeated or killed.

This is what one chief said after his tribe was driven off its land:

> Since our forefathers once saw the white man, more than seven times ten winters (70 years), he has filled graves with our bones. His way is destruction. He spoils what the Spirit of this country made beautiful and clean . . . We thought he came from the light. But now he comes like the dusk of the evening, not the light of the morning . . . He promised to give us things which he knew he would never give us. And after the promises he threatened us, with his soldiers, his jails, his iron chains. He takes more and more, and he dirties what he does not take.

TAKE IT FROM HERE

1 Make a model tepee, or wigwam. Put a ring of Plasticine on a board, and insert sticks or twigs at regular intervals, tied at the top with string. Drape a half-circle shaped piece of cloth or paper around it. Paint an Amerindian design on it. The tepee was an easily transportable home.

2 Amerindians used to mark trails or tracks through the forest. Try making signs with twigs for straight on, left and right, and try them out with your friends.

3 With the things you have made so far, make a display of Amerindian culture and history. Draw some pictures to show the European conquests of South America and North America from an Amerindian point of view.

4 Imagine you are a journalist with the US cavalry. Write an account of an attack on an Indian encampment for your newspaper.

5 Find out what happened at the Battle of Little Bighorn.

The human cost

The European conquerors destroyed most of the people they found in America – mainly through disease which they brought from Europe, against which the local people had no resistance. But they also killed many deliberately, and some of the inhabitants committed suicide through despair.

Within 30 years of Columbus's first landing, the Hispaniola population of 100,000 was completely wiped out. In Mexico, the Aztec Kingdom population fell from about 25 million in 1519 to only 2.6 million in 1568.

The main killer diseases were smallpox, measles and influenza. But there were cases of mass killings, and mass suicides in despair and protest against the barbarity of the Europeans.

When they ran short of local slaves, the Europeans brought black slaves from Africa to work for them. That is why there are so many black people of African origin in America today.

In North America, the Amerindian tribes were forced off their lands by trickery and violence. By 1870, the Indian way of life, which had developed over 30,000 years, was almost completely destroyed. Of 600 tribes recorded in 1800, only 250 were still in existence by 1900.

In some places, the United States forces deliberately killed whole tribes. As a result of its treatment, much of the native American population died out. Survivors were forcibly settled on **reservations**, usually areas of land too poor for white farming.

Although they were the original inhabitants of North America, the United States only

Black slaves brought from Africa to America

allowed the native Americans to become
United States citizens in 1924, and only
allowed them the full citizen's right of voting
in elections in 1948 – just 44 years ago.

 TAKE IT FROM HERE

1 Find out what it might be like to be a slave
with no will of your own. Offer your slave
services to your Mum or Dad for an hour.
(They will be pleased!)

2 Write to the Anti-Slavery Society, 180
Brixton Road, London SW9, and ask what
it does.

3 Find out where else in the world the
European settlers deliberately destroyed
the inhabitants.

4 Go to your junior library and ask to borrow
a book on the native Americans (or
Amerindians) of North America.

5 Make a display of the wars between the
white settlers and native Americans (Red
Indians) in the United States. See how
many native American tribes and famous
chiefs you can find out about.

Index

Acknowledgments

The Publishers would like to thank the following for their permission to reproduce copyright photographs in this book: The Ancient Art and Architecture Collection – pp2b.; 11t.; 18/19 Arxiu Mass – p6t. Bibliotheca Medicea Laurenziana – p24 Bibliothèque Nationale – pp4; 5 Bridgeman Art Library p16 British Library – p22 Bruce Coleman – p31b. The Hutchison Library – pp26l.; 27 Museum für Völkerkunde, Vienna – p25 National Maritime Museum, London – pp4t.; 4b.; 6b.; 7; 15r.; Peter Newark's American Pictures – pp1; 10b.; 29b; 30 Peter Newark's Western Americana – pp17b.; 29t.; 31t. Pierpont Morgan Library, New York PML 19921 – p9 Royal Geographical Society – pp23; 26r. Universitätsbibliothek Heidelberg – p21 University Museum of National Antiquities, Oslo, Norway – p20(both) U.S.T.T.A. – p2t

British Library Cataloguing in Publication Data
McDowall, David, 1945–
  Christopher Columbus project book.
  1. Exploration, history
  I. Title
  970.015

ISBN 0 340 52780 3

First published 1991

© 1991 David McDowall

Typeset by Litho Link Ltd, Welshpool, Powys.
Printed in Hong Kong for Hodder and Stoughton Educational, a division of Hodder and Stoughton Ltd, Mill Road, Dunton Green, Sevenoaks, Kent by Colorcraft Ltd.